Joseph Smith

The Boy . . . The Prophet

Joseph Smith

The Boy . . . The Prophet

Jay A. Parry/Steve Songer

Stonewell Press

Appreciation is expressed to the following for their assistance on this book:

To Kurt Hanks and Larry Belliston for information planning, to David Bartholomew for production artwork, and to Richard Moore for research.

This book was developed in conjunction with Information Design, Inc.

Reprint 2019 by Stonewell Press,
Salt Lake City, Utah

Library of Congress Catalog Number: 81-65790
ISBN: 978-1-62730-119-0

Contents

Introduction

When Joseph Smith was a boy, he looked just like all other boys. He played the same games they did. He helped with the work around the house and on his father's farm.

If you had lived near him he probably would have been your friend.

But Joseph was different in some ways because when he grew older Heavenly Father called him to be His prophet. And then he became God's friend.

This is the story of Joseph Smith, the boy and the prophet.

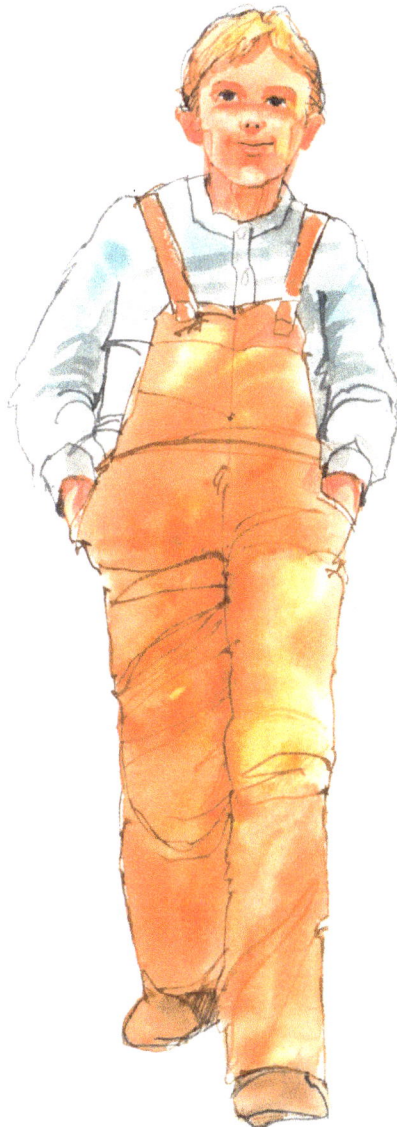

Joseph's Mother and Father

When Joseph was born, his mother and father were very poor. They had to work hard just to get food for their family, and they rarely had money left for luxuries. Life was always difficult, summer and winter.

Then things got worse. Joseph's father was a farmer, and for three years in a row his crops wouldn't grow. One year it failed to rain, and they suffered severe drought. Another year the weather was unusually cold, and the frost killed their plants.

Finally things got so bad that the family had to move to another town to try to start anew. Joseph's father opened a store that sold baked goods and root beer, while his mother painted coverings for furniture. At the same time they tried to start a new farm.

From dawn to dusk his parents worked, though even then they couldn't afford a nice house. But they were rich in other ways—they had a lot of children, and they knew the joy that comes from doing right. Those things made them happier than money ever would have done.

At the same time Joseph's father worked in his store, he began to clear trees off his new farm so he could plant crops. Joseph's mother helped in the store by making pies and other pastries.

2

Joseph's Leg Operation

Young Joseph was strong and healthy. He liked to play outside, to run and wrestle with his brothers. But when he was seven he came down with a very bad fever. It made him so weak that he wasn't able to get out of bed, or even to feed himself. His hand shook when he tried to use a spoon, and his mother and father had to pile quilts on top of him to keep him warm.

Finally the fever broke, and he was able to take care of himself again. But only for a short time. Then the sickness spread down to his leg, and it became infected. The leg swelled up bigger and bigger, causing Joseph so much pain that he finally cried out, "I can't stand it anymore!"

"I know, Joseph, I know," his mother answered, her brow furrowed with worry. She stroked his hair, comforting him.

She began to carry him around the house so he wouldn't be all alone in his room, trying to help him feel better. But then she became sick, and she couldn't take care of him anymore. "I'm sorry, Joseph," she said, kneeling by his bed and whispering against his cheek. "But I just don't have the strength any longer." So Joseph's big brother Hyrum helped while their father went to work. Hyrum sat by Joseph's bed all day, talking to him and pressing his sore leg between his hands so it wouldn't hurt so much.

When the doctor came to look at the swollen leg, he shook his head and pursed his lips. "This is very bad," he said. "*Very* bad." But doctors then didn't have the skills or medicines of today's doctors, so he didn't have any real solution. Finally he decided to try draining the infection from the leg.

He took out a very sharp knife and made a long cut on the bottom part of Joseph's leg. "This should help," he said, wiping the knife blade clean.

It did help for a while, but then Joseph's leg grew worse than before. The doctor cut his leg again, this time all the way down to the bone. Joseph nearly fainted from the pain of the knife. But again the treatment helped for only a short while.

By this time Joseph was weak and exhausted from the pain and lack of sleep.

"What can we do for him?" his parents asked each other. He was so sick he might even die! They prayed that the Lord would preserve Joseph's life.

The doctor was worried too. "I don't know what else to do," he admitted. "I can't just keep cutting his leg!" Finally he called in several other doctors to get their advice. They examined Joseph's leg, then met together to discuss it. They finally agreed there was only one solution.

"Joseph's leg is badly diseased," they told Mrs. Smith. "If we don't cut off his leg, the sickness will spread to the rest of his body, and he will die. Cutting off his leg is the only answer."

The pain was very intense when the doctor cut into Joseph's leg. But Joseph was brave, and he wouldn't let them tie him down.

Joseph's mother was horrified. "But if you do that, he can't walk!" she said. "He'll never be able to run and play again." Her eyes searched theirs. "You've got to try again," she pleaded. "Won't you please try just one more time?"

The doctors talked about it in low tones. Finally they decided they could.

Joseph looked up anxiously when they came into his room. His face was white with suffering, and his voice was weak. "You haven't come to cut off my leg, have you?" he asked.

"No," the doctor said. "We're not going to cut off your leg."

Joseph closed his eyes in relief. But then the head doctor, Dr. Stone, had some ropes brought in. "We're going to tie you up, Joseph," he said. "Otherwise you'll kick your leg in pain when I cut into it. I might slice into you deeper, by accident, and make things much worse."

Joseph shook his head. "No, Dr. Stone. If you won't tie me, I promise I'll hold still."

The doctor frowned as he thought, then said, "Well, if you won't let me tie you, at least drink some wine to help you relax."

"No!" Joseph said, very firmly. He licked his dry lips and stared up at the doctor. "I won't drink any wine, and I won't let you tie me down. Just let my father hold me, and I'll be all right." Then he looked at his mother, and tears were in her eyes. "Mother," he said, "please leave the room so you won't see the operation. But don't worry—the Lord will help me, and I'll get through it."

His mother left, and the doctors began the operation. First they made a deep cut into the flesh and drilled into the bone; then they began to break off pieces of the diseased bone. The pain was too great to stand, and Joseph screamed and screamed until his throat was sore.

When she heard his agony, Joseph's mother ran back into the room. She saw Joseph lying pale on the bed, his leg cut and bleeding. Blood was oozing from the hole, soaking into the bed sheets. Large drops of sweat were falling from his face.

"Oh, Joseph!" she exclaimed. But one of the doctors took her by the arm and helped her back out of the room.

When the operation was over, they cleaned up the bed and wiped all the blood away. They put away their tools and surgical instruments. Then they let Joseph's mother back into the room. She ran to the bed and held Joseph in her arms. "Joseph, Joseph," she said. He clung tightly to her and didn't say a word. His father stood behind the bed, his face drawn with worry.

But the operation worked. Joseph's leg began to improve, and soon he was able to get around again. He had to use crutches for quite a while, and he always had a limp. But the Lord had blessed him, and his leg had been spared.

During the operation, Joseph showed that he could be brave and strong. That was the kind of boy Heavenly Father needed in restoring the Church. When he grew older, Joseph would have to do many hard things—and God knew he would be ready.

Joseph's Family

Joseph's family had thirteen people: the mother and father, and eight boys and three girls. Here's a picture of what Joseph's family might have looked like when Joseph was eight. The numbers tell how old each person was:

Mother (Lucy), 38

William, 2

Father (Joseph Sr.), 42

Alvin, 15

Sophronia, 10

Hyrum, 14

Catherine, 1

Samuel, 5

Joseph, 8

Four children are not shown in the picture. The first boy born, who was never named, died when he was still a baby. Another boy was born between Samuel and William. He was named Ephraim, and he also died when he was a baby. Two children, Don Carlos and Lucy, were born to the family after Catherine. They're not shown in the picture because they hadn't been born yet when Joseph was eight.

The Smith Farm

Joseph lived on many farms while he was growing up. The one he remembered best was in Manchester near the little town of Palmyra, New York. When the family bought the farm, it was mostly covered with brush and trees. Joseph and his brothers and father put in many long hours clearing the ground and planting wheat and other grains.

Their first home on their Manchester farm was a very small log cabin—it had only two rooms on the main floor. Those rooms served as their kitchen and eating and living areas, and some of the family slept there as well. Up in the attic were two more small bedrooms.

Their living conditions, like most people's back then, were rather primitive compared to ours. The cabin floor was dirt, and they cooked their food in the fireplace. Their only light at night came from the fireplace, from candles, and from oil lanterns.

Even though they didn't have light switches or refrigerators, Joseph and his family were probably a lot like you and your family. They laughed and played together. They read in the Bible together. And every night they knelt on rugs on their cabin floor and had a family prayer together.

After the family moved to Manchester, they first lived in a small log cabin. They gradually cut the trees off the land so they could farm it, and later they built a larger home across the road.

The larger home Joseph's father and his boys built.

The first log cabin the Smiths lived in.

The Sacred Grove.

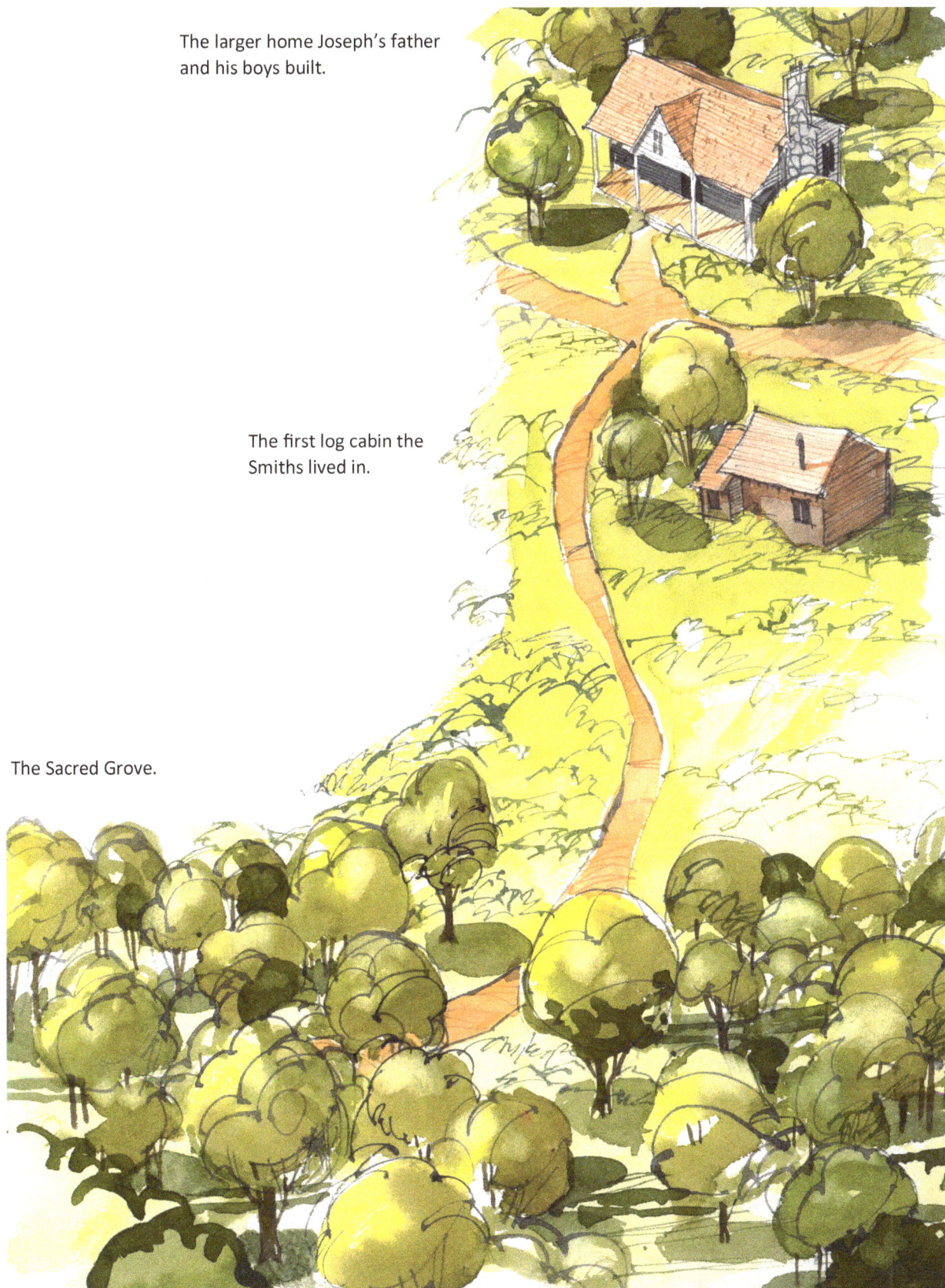

The First Vision

When Joseph was a young teenager, the people in his area became very excited about religion. Ministers set up tents or special platforms to preach their ideas about God, and the people flocked to hear them. Joseph and his family often went as well.

"Come to my church," one of the preachers would say. "It's the only true one on the earth."

"No!" another would shout. "Mine is the only church that has the truth!"

Then Joseph would visit a third. "It doesn't matter which church you join," the minister said. "All you need to do is live a good life."

It was all very confusing. Joseph wanted to go to the right church so he could feel closer to God, but he wasn't sure which church he should join. And the more he listened to the ministers, the more uncertain he became.

Joseph's family liked to read the Bible together, and Joseph learned to love the things it taught him. By the time he was fourteen he was reading it by himself. One night while he was reading in the book of James, he read these words:

"If any of you lack wisdom, let him ask of God, that giveth to all men liberally, and upbraideth not; and it shall be given him.

"But let him ask in faith, nothing wavering. For he that wavereth is like a wave of the sea driven with the wind and tossed."

"If any of you lack wisdom," it said, "let him ask of God . . . and it shall be given him."

A thrill swelled through Joseph's heart. God was promising him an answer to his question!

"If ever anyone needed wisdom," Joseph said to himself, "I certainly do!" He lay back on his bed and thought about it. He thought about it all the next day while he worked, and again the next. Finally he knew what he should do. He had been cutting wood in a grove a little way from their cabin. It was quiet and peaceful there. He would go there in the morning and ask God which church to join.

The next morning was a beautiful day. The sun was warm, and the sky was a rich blue. It was spring, and the birds chirped happily in the trees. Joseph got up early and walked out to the grove, his mind filled with what James had promised in the Bible. Praying had to be the answer. Only God could know for sure which church was right—and He would help Joseph know.

When Joseph reached the grove, he looked around to make sure no one was near. Then he knelt on the ground and tried to pray out loud. He had scarcely begun when thick darkness gathered around him, and an evil power tried to overcome him. It pushed against his tongue; it filled his throat. He couldn't speak. It was hard to even think. He struggled against it. The darkness filled his body. He panted, sweating. He tried to take a breath and couldn't. No sound would come from his mouth. He was certain he was going to die.

But he kept trying to pray. And then, just as suddenly as it had come, the darkness was gone. Satan had tried to keep Joseph from praying, but Joseph had continued to try, and now he was able speak the words of his prayer.

He had just begun to speak when he saw a light coming down from the sky. It was so bright he could barely look at it; it was brighter than the sun. The light came down through the trees, and Joseph was sure it would set them afire. But it didn't. It passed through the new spring leaves without harming them and finally rested upon Joseph.

Then he saw two Personages within the light. They were shaped like men, dressed in white and shining bright. They looked like angels, only more beautiful. One of them spoke. "Joseph," he said, and His voice was wonderful to hear.

"Joseph, this is my Beloved Son."

He pointed to the other Personage. "Hear Him!"

Then Joseph knew that the two Personages were Heavenly Father and Jesus Christ. Jesus told Joseph not to join any of the churches, saying that none of them was His true church.

Joseph's heart swelled with joy to talk to Jesus Himself and to be kneeling before God the Father. He had expected some kind of answer to his prayer—but a personal visit was more than he had ever dared dream!

Jesus told Joseph many things, and then He and His Father left. Joseph's strength gave out, and he fell to the ground, fainting from what he had seen and heard. When he woke again he was lying on his back in the grass. Birds rustled the leaves over his head. The light was gone. But only from the grove — never from Joseph's memory.

What Joseph Learned from the Vision

After the vision, Joseph was so weak he couldn't get up from the ground. But when he felt stronger he stood up and began to walk home, hardly noticing the warm spring sun pressing down on him. He didn't feel the stones under his feet. All he could think about was the vision God had just blessed him with. Here are some of the things he may have thought:

God loves *me*. He *knows* me. He visited me and called me by my name.

Satan is real. And very evil and powerful. He doesn't want us to pray, because he knows that will help us grow closer to God.

The ministers have been teaching that God is an invisible Spirit who fills the universe. They preach that Heavenly Father and Jesus are really the same person. But now I know they're wrong. I saw *two people!* And I saw that they have bodies shaped just liked mine.

The ministers told me that God doesn't speak to man anymore. But He spoke to me!

And He told me the true church isn't on the earth anymore. I shouldn't join any church.

After Joseph got home, he went to the fireplace and, leaning on the mantlepiece, told his mother what had happened. Her heart was filled with joy at what God had shown him, just as Joseph's was. For many weeks he felt the strong love of Jesus in his soul.

What Is a Prophet?

Joseph Smith was chosen by God to be a prophet. What did Joseph do that made him a prophet?

He taught us the truth about God. Most of the ministers were teaching the people that God is invisible, and that He's so large that He fills the entire universe. But Joseph Smith learned that God looks like a glorious man. That's one of the truths he taught us about God.

He talked with God. And often he heard the voice of God speaking back to him. God gave Joseph many important things to tell the people. And He sent many angels to give Joseph other instructions.

He told us the words of God. Joseph often told the people things that God wanted them to know. He told them about building temples, about paying tithing, and about the importance of having the priesthood. We wouldn't know about those things without Joseph Smith, the Prophet.

He told us about things that would happen in the future. Many years before it happened, Joseph told the people about the American Civil War. He prophesied that the Latter-day Saints would go to the Rocky Mountains as pioneers, several years before it happened. He told the people that Jesus would be coming again, and that those who are righteous will be able to live with Him.

One of the most important things the Prophet Joseph did was *translate the Book of Mormon,* which is another testament of Jesus Christ. The angel Moroni came to him one night and told him about the golden plates. Those plates contained many of the words of God, Moroni explained, and the angel said that if Joseph was righteous he would be able to give those words to all the world.

Joseph *was* righteous. And now, because of him, people throughout the world, in many different languages, have God's words as they are found in the Book of Mormon. And because of that, they can know much more about the love and sacrifice of Jesus Christ, our Savior.

Alvin's Death

Alvin was Joseph's oldest brother. Even though he was seven years older than Joseph, they were very close and loved each other very much. Two months after the angel Moroni visited Joseph, Alvin grew very ill—so ill that he knew he was going to die.

After a few days, Alvin called his brothers and sisters in to his bedside. First he spoke to Hyrum, who was more than a year younger than he was. "Take good care of Mother and Father," he said. "Don't let them work too hard, because they're getting old."

Then he turned to Sophronia. "Help Mother around the house," he said. "And do the things for Father that he needs."

But he saved his most important instruction for Joseph. "Be a good boy," he said, "and do everything you can to get the golden plates. Obey the things God tells you to do. And set a good example for the younger children."

Alvin died soon after that. Everyone in the whole neighborhood was sad, because Alvin had been such a good young man. But the family missed him most of all. For a long time after that, whenever they thought of him they would cry, because he wasn't with them anymore.

Many years later, Joseph still remembered his feelings for Alvin. "I was so sad when Alvin died," he said. "I thought my heart would almost burst."

After the Kirtland Temple was built, Joseph saw a marvelous vision of heaven. He saw Heavenly Father and Jesus on a glorious throne. He saw Adam and Abraham. And there was his beloved brother Alvin.

The Lord explained how Alvin could be there, even though he had never been baptized. God will bless us for the good desires of our hearts, he said, and He will provide a way for all those who love Him to be with Him again.

Two months before Alvin died, Joseph was visited by an angel named Moroni. Joseph had been praying in his bedroom late one night when Moroni appeared in the room. He was dressed all in white, and he was so bright that a light seemed to come from him. He told Joseph about the golden plates and gave him other instructions. He explained that Joseph was to translate the plates. Then he left.

While Joseph lay thinking about the angel's visit, Moroni came again and repeated his instructions. He came a third time that night, then once again in the morning.

And every year after that, until Joseph was given the plates, Moroni met him on the side of the hill where the plates were buried. There he taught him and prepared him for his important missions of translating the Book of Mormon and becoming a prophet of God.

Protecting the Plates

Four years after Alvin died, the angel Moroni gave Joseph the plates. That same day, Satan sent some of his evil spirits to try to keep Joseph from taking the plates home. Satan knew the Book of Mormon would bring people closer to God, and that thought made him angry.

Along with his evil spirits, Satan inspired wicked men to try to stop Joseph. He whispered to them that the plates were made of gold, and that with the gold they could become very rich. But Moroni had given Joseph a promise: "If you will remain humble and obedient," he said, "God will protect the plates."

Joseph resisted the evil spirits, and he was able to keep out of sight of the wicked men and hide the plates in a hollow log in the woods. The next day he went to work digging a well for some people several miles away.

The sword of Laban.

Joseph rolled away a stone to find the plates.

The plates were stored in a stone box.

While he was working, some of his neighbors made plans to steal the plates. They hired a man who claimed secret powers to tell them by magic where the plates were. "Young Joe thinks he's hidden them," they gloated. "But our man can tell us where to look!"

Joseph's father heard about their plans and grew very worried. He sent a message to Joseph. "You must rush home," the message said. "They're going to get the plates!"

When Joseph got the news, he borrowed a horse and hurried home. He went out to the hollow log—the plates were still safe! He hid them under his clothes and started back home, walking through the woods and fields so he wouldn't be seen.

Men chased Joseph through the woods, trying to get the plates from him.

But the people found him anyway. Men jumped on Joseph three different times, flailing at him and trying to push him down and take the plates away.

But Joseph was too strong for them. He struggled with each man until he was able to knock him back, and then he ran on.

Finally he got home, exhausted from the effort. "Quick, Carlos," he said to a younger brother, panting, "get a special box to put the plates in!" Carlos found a strong wooden box, and they put the plates inside, then hid them safely in the house.

Not too many days later, they heard that a mob was coming to get the plates. "The hiding place isn't good enough," Joseph decided. "We've got to find a new one." He went to the fireplace, pulled up the stones in the floor, and dug a hole in the dirt. Then he put the plates in the hole and returned the stones to their places.

He had scarcely finished when the mob came. Joseph ran to the door and threw it open. "Come on, men, let's get them!" he shouted to his brothers behind him, pretending that a crowd of men was in the house with him.

The mob was fooled by his trick. "He's got an army in there!" one shouted. "With guns!" Frightened, the mob scattered. They didn't return that day.

But a short time later Joseph felt another mob was coming. He took the plates out from under the stones and took them to a shop across the street. "We'll hide the plates under some grain in the loft," Joseph told his family. "And we'll put the box under the floor, empty. Don't worry—the plates will be safe."

That night the mob came. They broke down the door of the shop and ripped up the floor. When they found the box, empty, they angrily broke it into pieces and threw the remnants around the room. But they couldn't find the golden plates.

Evil people tried many other times to get the plates from Joseph. They attacked him, shot at him, and attacked his house. But because Joseph was righteous, God protected the plates, just as He had promised.

21

But finally it was too much. "I can't get any translating done," Joseph complained. "The mobs won't leave me alone. We've got to leave the area." He and his new wife, Emma, gathered their clothes and some food and packed them all on a wagon. Last of all, Joseph brought out the plates, wrapped in cloth, and buried them in the bottom of a barrel of beans.

"God bless you!" he called to his family. He clucked at the horse and began to drive away. They had barely left when they were stopped by a wicked sheriff. "You've left some debts back there in town," the sheriff lied. "But if you'll just pay me the money, there won't be any trouble."

"I don't have any money," Joseph said. "And I don't have any debts."

When Joseph needed to take the plates to another town, he hid them in a barrel of beans.

The sheriff's eyes glinted. "Oh, yes," he said, his voice low. "You've got debts. And I guess I'll just have to take something off your wagon to pay for them." He began to look through Joseph's and Emma's things, trying to find the plates. But he didn't look in the barrel of beans, and finally he left, empty-handed.

Joseph and Emma drove on down the road. But the sheriff stopped them again. "You must have *something* I can take for your debts," he said. He searched the wagon again—but not the barrel of beans. Finally, discouraged, he rode away.

Joseph urged the horse on faster, and finally he got the plates safely away. In his new home he was able to find more time. With the power of God, he was able to translate the words on the plates into the Book of Mormon.

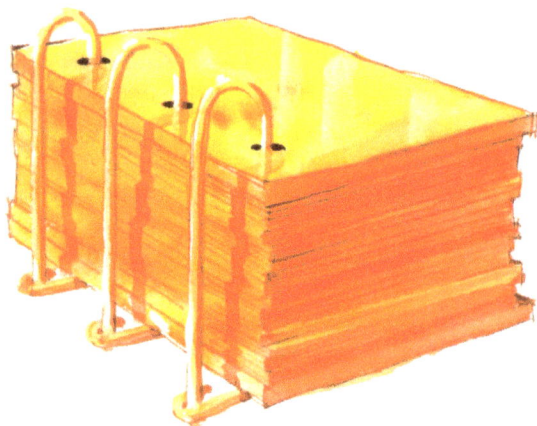

Because Joseph protected the plates so well, we're able to read about the Nephites and the Lamanites today, and about how much God loved them and how much He loves us.

The gold in the plates was worth a lot of money. But the Book of Mormon that came from them is worth much, much more than any money.

When Joseph translated the plates, he read out loud to a helper, who wrote the words down on sheets of paper. While Joseph was translating, he wasn't supposed to show the plates to anyone else. At the beginning, he hung a curtain or blanket between him and his helper. Later he just wrapped them in a small tablecloth and left them sitting on the table while he worked.

Eventually, an angel showed the plates to three other men, and the Lord told Joseph to show them to eight others. These men were called "witnesses" of the Book of Mormon, and their testimony is written in every copy printed.

Joseph's Wife and Children

When Joseph was a young man, he had to move away from home to find work. One year he stayed with a family named Hale, while he worked near their house.

The Hales had a beautiful daughter named Emma, and it wasn't too long before she and Joseph fell in love. Emma was tall and had dark eyes and black hair. She was a very good housekeeper and cook, and she sang in the village choir.

After they had courted for a while, Joseph and Emma decided to get married. But Emma's parents didn't like the idea—they didn't believe Joseph when he told them of his vision of God.

Since the Hales didn't approve of their wedding, Joseph and Emma went to a nearby town and got married on their own. Then they went to live with Joseph's parents, and Joseph farmed with his father.

Joseph and Emma had many children. Joseph loved children very much, but most of their children died, one by one, causing them much sorrow.

Their first child, named Alvah, died just a few hours after he was born.

Then Emma had twins; they named them Thaddeus and Louisa. These also died, only three hours after their birth. Emma cried and cried; she couldn't be comforted.

Then Joseph learned that another woman in town had died that same day — right after having twins. He and Emma adopted those twins to be their own children. They were named Joseph and Julia. Unfortunately, baby Joseph died a year later, but Julia grew to be an adult.

Their next three children were all boys. They were named Joseph, Frederick, and Alexander. These boys brought Joseph and Emma much joy all through their lives.

Their next two boys didn't live, though. The first one was named Don Carlos. He died when he was a year old. The second one died before he was even born.

Joseph and Emma had one last child, born after Joseph died. His name was David. Joseph never got to see David in this life, but surely he was very happy in the spirit world when he knew that Emma had another baby to love.

When Joseph and Emma met, they quickly fell in love. And even though they were persecuted because of Joseph's vision, they had much joy together.

The
Church Begins

When Heavenly Father and Jesus came to Joseph Smith in the grove, Jesus told Joseph not to join any church. None of them was true, He said.

After that Joseph didn't have a church to go to. But his family did read the Bible, and they had regular family prayers.

Then, ten years later, the Lord spoke to Joseph and told him that He was going to restore His church to the earth again. And He wanted Joseph to be the one to help Him do it.

The Church was formed in 1830
in a log cabin in New York state.

The first thing the Church needed was the priesthood. So God sent John the Baptist and then Peter, James, and John to give the priesthood to Joseph.

Next, the Church needed members. So in April 1830 Joseph and about fifty other people met in a log house to officially start the Church. Six people were chosen to be the first members of the Church. They took the sacrament and then were all baptized. Then some of the others were baptized and became members too. The Holy Ghost visited many that day, and everyone present felt the love of God.

The next thing the Church needed was leaders. Joseph Smith was named as the first elder of the Church. Oliver Cowdery, who had helped by writing the words as Joseph translated the Book of Mormon, was named the second elder. Later, the Lord told Joseph to ordain twelve men to be apostles of Jesus Christ. Joseph also followed the Lord's instructions to send out missionaries.

Those missionaries were the first of many thousands who have helped the Church grow bigger and bigger—from only six people to many million.

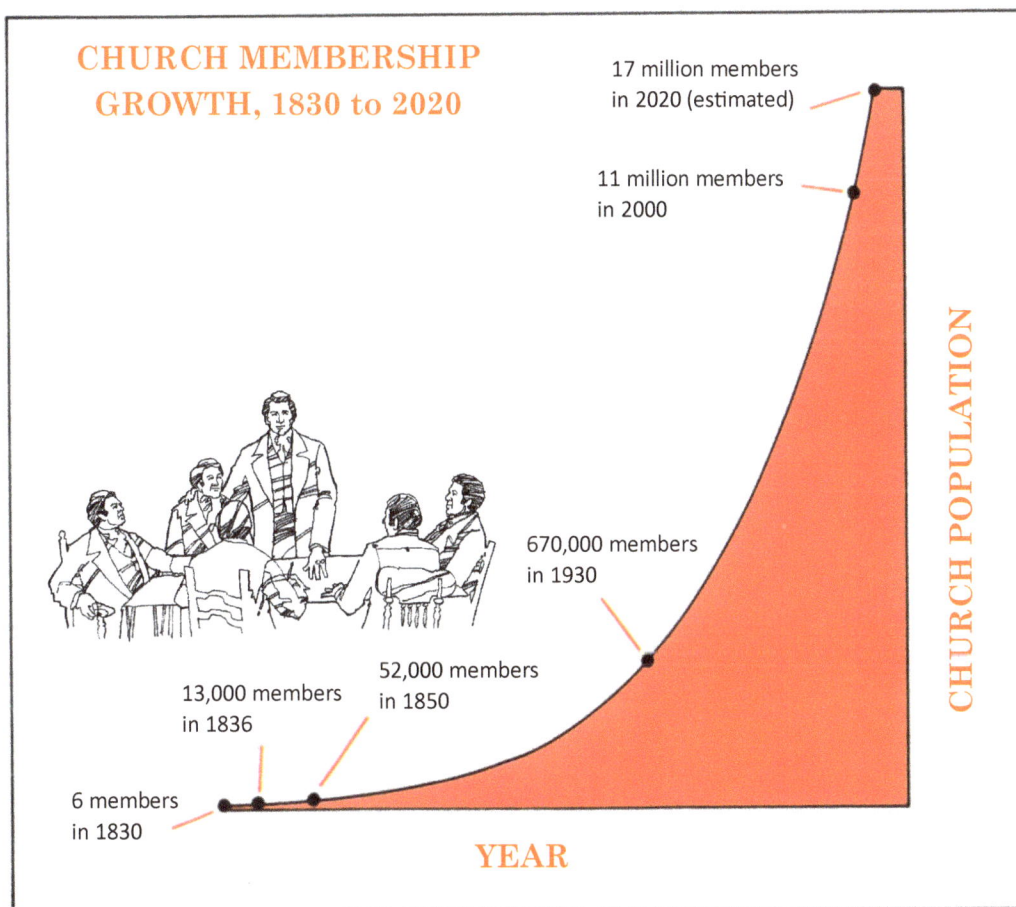

CHURCH MEMBERSHIP GROWTH, 1830 to 2020

17 million members in 2020 (estimated)

11 million members in 2000

CHURCH POPULATION

670,000 members in 1930

52,000 members in 1850

13,000 members in 1836

6 members in 1830

YEAR

Millions of people have testimonies that Joseph Smith was a prophet of God. And every year many more join the church that God restored through Joseph.

Joseph Loved Children

Joseph loved to be around children. Often he took time to play with them when he was out visiting, doing the things they liked to do. The children learned to look forward to his visits.

One girl named Margarette McIntire Burgess remembered a time when the Prophet Joseph Smith helped her and her brother, Wallace. They were going to school, walking on a very muddy road, when they got stuck in the mud and couldn't get out. The more they tried to get loose, the more the mud held them tight. They grew very frightened, worried that they'd be stuck in the mud all day and all night—and they began to cry.

Then they looked up and saw Joseph coming. He pulled them out of the mud and put them on drier ground. He smiled warmly and cleaned the mud off their shoes, then took out his handkerchief and dried their eyes.

"It's all right," he said to them. "Don't worry. You'll be all right."

Margarette and Wallace felt much better then. They stopped crying and went safely on to school.

They never forgot how the Prophet had helped them. He was their friend, and they loved him.

Joseph loved to play with children—and to help them when they were in trouble.

Joseph Was Strong

Joseph Smith was a very strong man. He was good at wrestling—so good, in fact, that other men often liked to challenge him to a wrestling match. Then they'd pick out the very best wrestler in their town, trying to find someone who could beat Joseph. But some of Joseph's friends said that he never was beaten in wrestling.

Joseph's strength helped him many times when mobs attacked him. Sometimes two or three or even more men would grab him at the same time, trying to hold him down. But because Joseph was strong and fast, he was usually able to fight them off and get away from them.

One day he was with his cousin John when a mob attacked. John and Joseph ran through the woods and swamps to get away—until John, sick and exhausted, couldn't run any farther. "Go ahead and leave me here," John said. "I'll be all right."

But Joseph couldn't leave him to the mob. So he picked John up on his broad shoulders and carried him on through the woods. They traveled that way for several hours, until Joseph himself was exhausted. But still he continued on, carrying his cousin on his back, until at last they escaped the mob and were safe again.

Cousin John was big and heavy, but Joseph carried him through the swamp for several hours.

Saving
the Stagecoach

Once Joseph was riding a stagecoach to Washington, D.C., on his way to visit the president of the United States. Before they arrived, the coach driver stopped at a tavern to get a drink. Something spooked the horses, and they began to run wildly down the road.

The passengers began to grow very frightened. "The horses will tip the coach over and kill us all!" one man exclaimed.

At that, the eyes of one of the women grew wide. "It will crush my little baby!" she said. She began to shove the baby out of the window to drop him onto the ground. "I'll save his life!" she shouted.

But Joseph grabbed her arm. "Don't do that!" he said, his voice urgent. "Your baby could die when he hits the ground. Maybe I can stop the coach."

He told the other passengers to wait quietly, and then he opened the door and began to climb up the side of the stagecoach. It careened down the road with such speed that Joseph began to wonder if he'd made the right decision. Then it bumped over a rock, and he almost fell off. But he clung tightly to the side of the coach and finally got onto the driver's seat. He grabbed the reins and finally pulled the horses to a stop.

He was sweating and his heart was racing when he stepped down and helped the people out of the coach. They were very grateful. "You were so brave," said one. "You saved our lives."

"Yes," said another, "you should be given a big reward."

Joseph *was* very brave. But he didn't want a reward. He was just happy he'd been able to help his fellow travelers.

If Joseph had not been so brave, he might not have tried to stop the horses. His courage helped him many times during his life.

The Healings at Montrose

One day the members of the Church in Nauvoo became very sick. It was a very difficult time: a lot of them had just arrived in town and didn't have houses to stay in. So Joseph brought several of them to stay in his house, while he moved into a tent in his yard.

Every day Joseph helped the sick. And each day he grew more and more tired as he helped others without getting much rest. It nearly made *him* sick.

One morning when Joseph got up he thought about how sick everyone was. "We've got to do something more," he said to himself. He knelt and prayed, asking for help. Then the power of God came to him, and he knew what to do. He went into his house and, using his priesthood, healed all the people there.

He walked down toward the river, healing everyone he met. Then he crossed the river to a place called Montrose. Many others were sick there; one by one he went to them and healed them.

Then he went into the house of Elijah Fordham. Elijah was almost dead—in fact, everyone thought he would die any minute. Joseph stood by him and took his hand. Elijah stirred.

"Elijah, do you know me?" Joseph asked. Elijah was so sick he couldn't think very well. He looked at Joseph with glassy eyes but didn't answer.

Joseph asked again, "Elijah, do you know me?"

With a very low whisper Elijah answered, "Yes."

"Do you think you can be healed?" Joseph asked.

"I'm afraid it is too late," Elijah said. "If you had come sooner, I think I might have been." His voice was very weak.

But Joseph knew the power of the priesthood, and he knew it wasn't too late. "Do you believe that Jesus is the Christ?" he asked.

"I do, Brother Joseph," Elijah answered.

Then Joseph spoke with a loud voice. "Elijah, I command you in the name of Jesus of Nazareth to arise and be well!"

The whole house seemed to shake. Elijah leaped quickly from his bed and got dressed. He ate a bowl of milk and bread; then he put on his hat and followed Joseph out into the street.

Joseph healed many others that day. Some were nearly dead when he reached them. But with his priesthood and faith in Jesus Christ, Joseph was able to save their lives.

Heavenly Father showed the people that He loved them and was aware of their suffering when He inspired Joseph to heal them with the power of the priesthood.

Joseph Is Killed

Wherever Joseph went, many people loved him. They knew he was telling the truth, and they wanted to be near him. They knew that the things he taught would help them to live with Heavenly Father and Jesus again.

But many people hated him. They knew their lives were wicked, and they didn't want to change. When Joseph told them to repent they grew angry.

So they tried to hurt him, hoping he'd stop preaching about God. Some tried to kill him. One night a mob dragged him from his home and pulled him into the dirt outside. One tried to pour some acid into his mouth. Another kicked him again and again, bruising his chest and sides. Then they pulled off his clothes and poured hot tar all over him. It burned his skin, and he screamed out with the pain.

They tried to harm him in other ways too. Many times they lied to the police so Joseph would be arrested for things he didn't do. He spent long months in crowded and dirty prisons because of those lies.

Once wicked men tortured Joseph by pouring hot tar over his skin. Then they put feathers on the tar to humiliate him.

After Joseph had been persecuted like this for many years, wicked men took him to a jail in Carthage, Illinois. They put him upstairs with his brother Hyrum and a few of his friends and held them prisoner.

The men had been in the jail for two days when a mob attacked. Joseph and Hyrum were trapped in the jail, and in just a few moments the mob had shot Hyrum on the side of his nose. He fell dead to the floor. Joseph ran to the window to see if he could jump to safety. But part of the mob was outside, and they shot him. He fell from the window to the ground, dead.

The Saints mourned deeply when they heard the news. Joseph was their leader. He was the one who gave them God's word. He loved them, and they loved him in return. But they knew that even though he was now dead his body would be resurrected, and he would live again. And they knew that if they were righteous, they could be with him when they were resurrected, and would again enjoy the friendship they had known.

Joseph Smith's Life

When Joseph died he was still a young man, only thirty-eight years old. Our other prophets have died much older, when they were seventy or eighty or ninety years old.

But Joseph accomplished a lot of things in his short life. He saw the Father and the Son when he was still a boy. He was visited by the angel Moroni, who gave him the golden plates. He translated the Book of Mormon for all the world to have, giving us much truth about Jesus Christ and His gospel.

He was visited by John the Baptist and by Peter, James, and John, who gave him the priesthood.

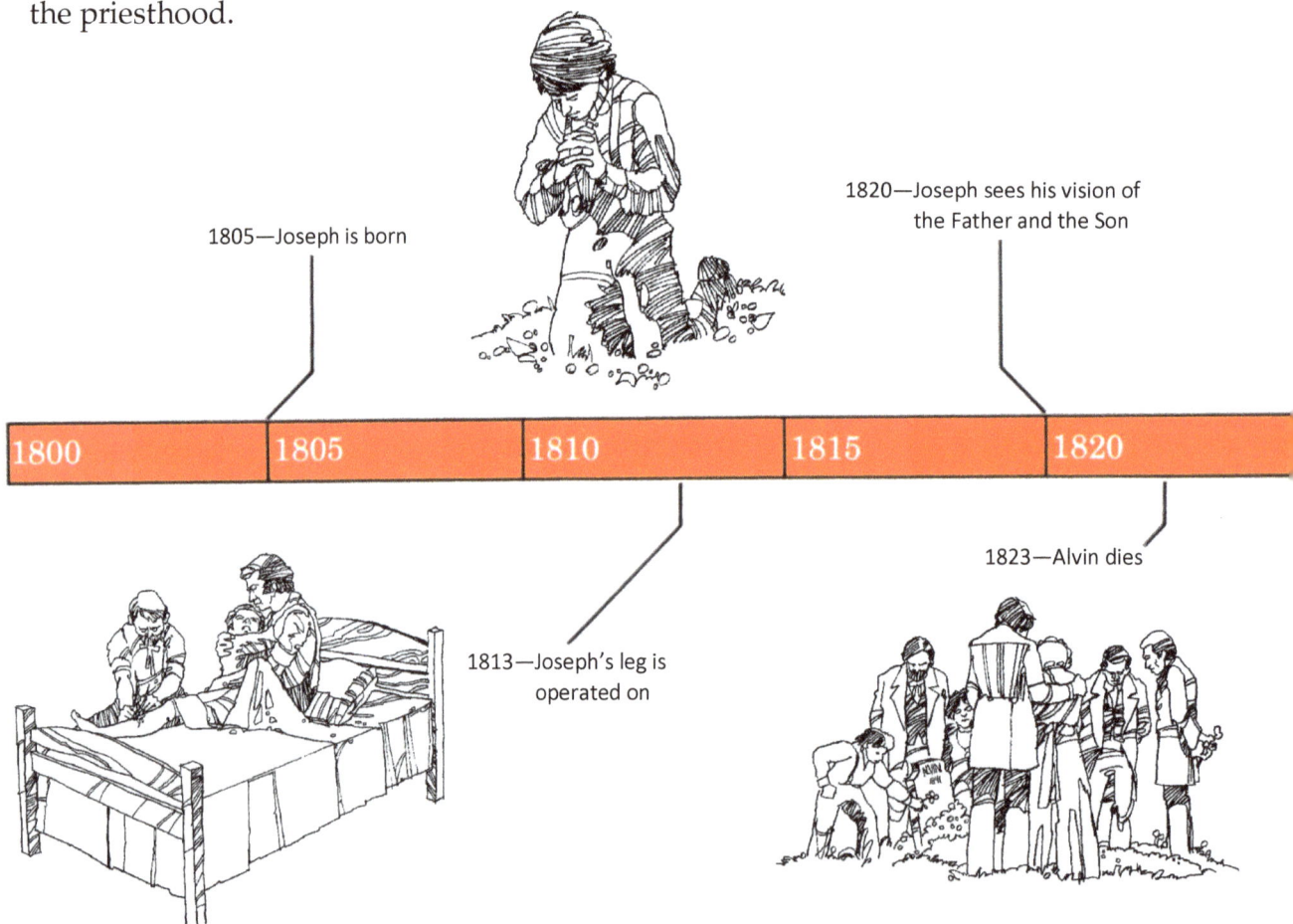

1805—Joseph is born

1820—Joseph sees his vision of the Father and the Son

1800	1805	1810	1815	1820

1823—Alvin dies

1813—Joseph's leg is operated on

Following God's instruction, he brought Jesus's true church back to the earth again.

He sent missionaries to many different countries to tell the people that the gospel of Jesus Christ had been restored to the earth.

He started a new city, named Nauvoo, in Illinois. He preached many wonderful sermons. After receiving directions from the Lord about how to build temples, Joseph had a temple built in Kirtland, Ohio, and started another in Nauvoo.

Joseph Smith was a general in an army. He ran for president of the United States.

He was the loving father of eleven children.

He earned the love of thousands of good people—and through the years those thousands have grown to many millions.

Joseph Smith was a true prophet of God. Throughout his life, in all he did, he followed Jesus Christ, and he always taught others to do the same.

1827—Moroni gives Joseph the golden plates

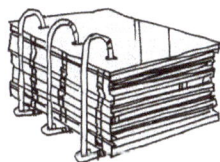

1830—Joseph organizes the true church

1844—Joseph is killed by a mob

| 1825 | 1830 | 1835 | 1840 | 1845 |

1827—Joseph and Emma are married

1839—Joseph saves the stagecoach

What Was Joseph Like?

Joseph Smith was a large man. He was more than six feet tall and weighed 200 pounds, and he was very strong. His eyes were blue, and his hair was light brown and wavy.

Joseph walked with a slight limp because of the leg operation he had when he was seven. One of his front teeth was chipped when a mob attacked him.

He was a very friendly man. He loved others, and most people liked him right away when they met him.

He liked to relax and play games. Sometimes he played ball with the younger boys, or he wrestled with the men and played a game called "pulling sticks."

He also spent time with his family. He took them to the circus, to music concerts, and for rides on a riverboat. Sometimes in the winter he took his children out to a pond and slid around on the ice with them.

But life wasn't all fun for Joseph. He spent many of his days doing hard work—and he enjoyed it. He labored at plowing fields, digging ditches, picking apples, cutting wood, and other kinds of work.

But most of the time he did God's work. He loved the Lord and loved to serve Him. The scriptures tell us that he did more to help mankind than any other person who ever lived on the earth, except for Jesus Christ Himself!

www.ingramcontent.com/pod-product-compliance
Lightning Source LLC
Chambersburg PA
CBHW060901090426
42738CB00025B/3490